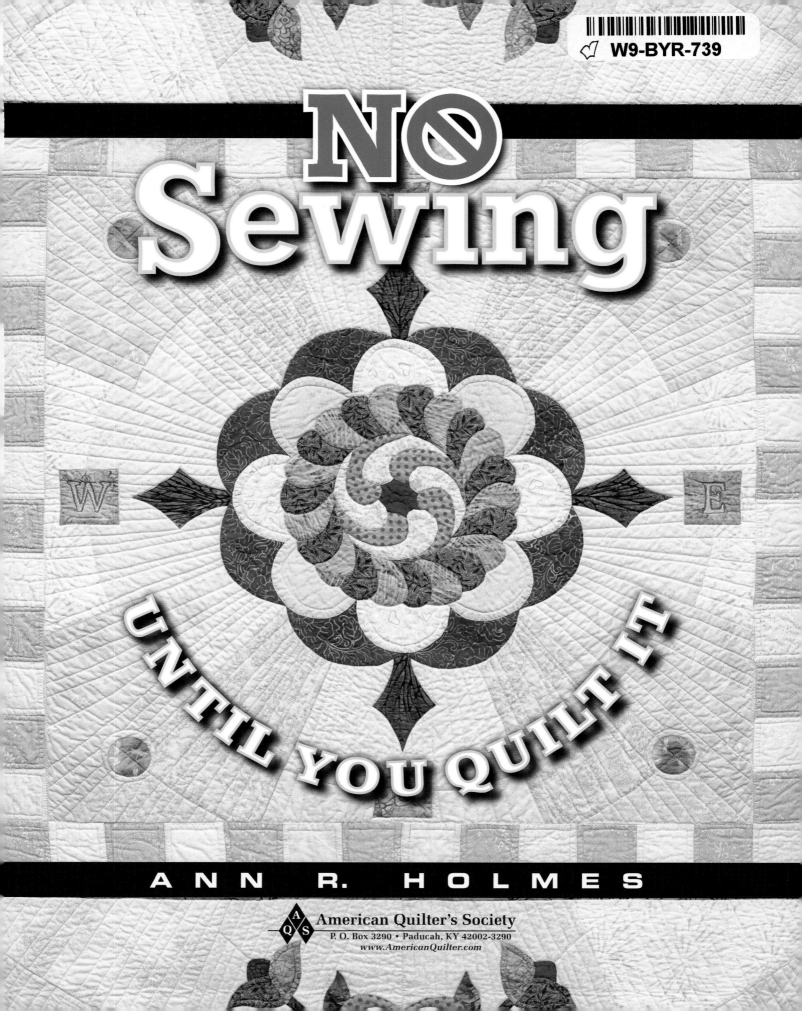

NO Sewing

UNTIL YOU QUILT IT

ANN R. HOLMES

American Quilter's Society
P. O. Box 3290 • Paducah, KY 42002-3290
www.AmericanQuilter.com

Located in Paducah, Kentucky, the American Quilter's Society (AQS) is dedicated to promoting the accomplishments of today's quilters. Through its publications and events, AQS strives to honor today's quiltmakers and their work and to inspire future creativity and innovation in quiltmaking.

EXECUTIVE BOOK EDITOR: ANDI MILAM REYNOLDS
SENIOR BOOK EDITOR: LINDA BAXTER LASCO
COPY EDITOR: CHRYSTAL ABHALTER
GRAPHIC DESIGN: ELAINE WILSON
ILLUSTRATIONS: LYNDA SMITH
COVER DESIGN: MICHAEL BUCKINGHAM
QUILT PHOTOGRAPHY: CHARLES R. LYNCH
HOW-TO PHOTOGRAPHY: ANN R. HOLMES

Additional copies of this book may be ordered from the American Quilter's Society, PO Box 3290, Paducah, KY 42002-3290, or online at www.AmericanQuilter.com.

Text © 2012, Author, Ann R. Holmes
Artwork © 2012, American Quilter's Society

LIBRARY OF CONGRESS CATALOGING-IN-PUBLICATION DATA
Holmes, Ann R., 1949-
  No sewing until you quilt it / by Ann R. Holmes.
    pages cm
  Summary: "Use the author's 7 patterns or create your own, try out fabrics on a forgiving fusible background, replace patches until you're satisfied, layer, and stitch. Ann's turned-edge technique gives an elegant look to any quilt. No more ripping out stitches because there's no sewing until you quilt"--Provided by publisher.
  ISBN 978-1-60460-021-6
  1. Patchwork--Patterns. 2. Machine quilting--Patterns. I. Title.
  TT835.H556234 2012
  746.46--dc23
                              2012010048

COVER: SUMMER'S END, detail. Full quilt on page 57.

TITLE PAGE: BLOOM WHERE YOU ARE PLANTED, detail. Full quilt on page 48.

THIS PAGE: SPRING LANDSCAPE, detail. Full quilt on pages 38–39.

Dedication

I dedicate this book to my granddaughter, Rebekah Joy, and to future quilters everywhere. To those who love fabric and quilts but say they can't quilt because they can't sew, this book is for you. And to experienced quilters who may find this a joyful approach to quiltmaking, welcome to the liberating world of "the no sew method" of creating a quilt.

Acknowledgments

I am thankful for the support of my family:

My husband, Bert, a scientist and teacher, is my greatest promoter. My daughter, Amy, with her intellectual spirit, has led me on adventures in foreign countries, most recently to Cairo, Egypt, where she is living and teaching at The American University. My son, Doug, an engineer and teacher, for his sustaining faith in God through difficult times, gives me courage that I should fear not.

I am thankful to the Asheville Quilt Guild in Asheville, North Carolina, where I was inspired by the many talented members and the wonderful teachers that came to our meetings, and to my Thursday Night Busy Bees: Dina Garland, Beverly Cutter, Sharon Killian, Kris Gowin Tarpley, Chris Cicotello, Amy Milne and her daughter Lil, who named us, for their constant encouragement.

This book would not have been possible without the generous support of Art House, my landlord in Arlington, Virginia, who offered me extra space for all my projects while we lived there on a temporary basis for three years while the bulk of this book was being written.

Helen McCarthy is my "go to girl" for quilt construction, proofreading, and editing.

Quilt construction assistance was also given by Julie Bagamary, Brian Fackler, Sara Hill, Marie Marcella, Diana Ramsey, and Rachael Smith.

Website and other technical assistance was given by Leah Day and Amy Milne. I am grateful to the American Quilter's Society for taking a chance on me, especially to Andi Reynolds and Linda Lasco and their teams.

It certainly took a small village to get this book to print and I am so thankful.

Contents

Left: Bloom Where You Are Planted, detail. Full quilt on page 48.

Introduction

Growing up near Lebanon, Pennsylvania, I would often stop to admire beautiful Amish quilts. They looked so perfect; it was amazing to find out that a humility block was added, as no one is perfect except God. This may be a legend, but that attitude is very healing for me. All my work is full of mistakes—I don't need to ADD a humility block. It taught me that I should just try and see what develops. My whole body of work is full of humility; I offer it that you might find courage to try your ideas and have fun in the process.

Perhaps you have a dream or a desire to create a special quilt. Martin Luther King, Jr., tells us: "Take the first step in faith. You don't have to see the whole staircase, just take the first step." Let's begin our journey of thinking outside the stitching line to build your dream quilt.

No Sewing Until You Quilt It is an easy technique, so relax. It is like going back to grade school where we get to play with fabric, glue, and paper. Once you learn the basic steps, you are on your way to building your own creations. I hope that you enjoy this as a fun and stress-free method of creating what your heart desires. So many of my students will tell me that they had a project in mind but did not know how to proceed. After they have taken my class they are inspired to try their own ideas. I hope that this book will inspire your future quilt possibilities.

No Sewing Until You Quilt It is a turned-edge appliqué technique using a fusible tricot interfacing as a foundation and glue stick on the seam allowances. There is NO sewing until AFTER you make your quilt sandwich; then you stitch-and-quilt all at the same time by machine with a free-motion or darning foot attached. This gives you freedom to create almost any shape and to edit

OPPOSITE: ORIENTAL IRIS TRIPTYCH, detail. Full quilt on pages 42–43.

your work without ripping out seams. Most of my quilts are then machine washed and dried to add texture and remove the glue. The technique works for wallhangings and soft bed quilts alike.

Fusible Tricot Interfacing

Why a fusible tricot interfacing and what is it? A tricot, one-sided fusible interfacing provides a foundation for building your quilt top. It holds the pieces in place until they are stitched down as they are quilted. It is soft, it drapes, and you can see through it when it is placed over your working drawing. It is also more forgiving than other fusible materials, allowing you to edit your work by gently pulling off pieces that you want to change.

There are several one-sided, fusible interfacing products that I am aware of: French Fuse, Fusi-Knit, and Pro-Sheer Elegance. They come in 22" and 60" widths in white, tan, and black. Tricot is made from polyester, rayon, and Lycra.

I use a white 60" wide French Fuse. Dressmakers have used it for many years in knits. Quilters have used it for T-shirt quilts as a stabilizer. It is suitable for lightweight woven fabrics like cotton. As this fusible will not shrink, I prewash my fabrics. Once your cotton pattern shapes or pieces are sealed down with an iron and you layer the finished top with batting and a prewashed backing fabric, it will not stretch, at least not more than the normal stretch of cotton on the crosswise grain, nor will your quilt shrink more than the batting that you have chosen.

Overview of the Two-Part Technique

PART 1: Build the Top

Start by printing the full-size pattern from the CD. This will be your working drawing. Make a complete copy on freezer paper. Lay one continuous piece of the fusible tricot interfacing over the working drawing with the adhesive or textured side up and build the pattern pieces on top, appliqué style, from background to foreground. The freezer-paper patterns are pressed onto the RIGHT side of the fabrics. (Unlike other freezer-paper techniques, the pattern pieces are NOT reversed.) You'll turn under the edges as you build, using a glue stick and a sealing iron. There's no sewing involved until you're ready to do the quilting.

PART 2: Stitch-and-Quilt

Make a quilt sandwich using a spray baste adhesive, layering the built top, batting, and backing. Now you can appliqué/stitch-and-quilt at the same time using either a straight or zigzag stitch with a free-motion foot. **You do not need to be an expert in machine quilting.** Even those who are uncomfortable with machine quilting may find this an enjoyable way to quilt.

The sometimes-daunting question of "How do I quilt the top?" is answered. You will know exactly how to proceed. The first step is to stitch around all the shapes to hold them in place with either a small zigzag or straight stitch. This outline stitching will make your design pop. Then use echo quilting around each shape or piece. Use invisible thread on the top, either clear or smoke, so you don't have to worry about perfect stitches; you are holding the quilt together and adding lovely texture at the same time.

Important Information

Tools and Supplies for the Working Drawing and Freezer-Paper Patterns

Paper

When you print out a pattern to size from the CD, that becomes your working drawing. When I draw original designs I use plain white paper for my working drawing. There are large tablets (27" x 32") available at office supply stores. They also have paper with 1" grids if you are going to design something with lots of straight lines. You can use clear tape to put pieces together if you need bigger paper. (The clear tape on the working drawing is protected from direct contact with the iron by the fusible and fabric of the quilt top.) Butcher paper is available at wholesale food distributors in 36" wide rolls; that's a lot of paper but very handy for the large projects that I do.

Freezer paper

Use freezer paper to make the patterns that will be ironed onto the RIGHT side of your fabrics. This paper is available at most grocery stores near the aluminum foil in 18" wide rolls. When you need a wider freezer paper, tape sheets together with masking tape. You can iron over the masking tape.

LEFT: RHODODENDRON BUD, detail, made by the author. Full quilt on CD.

Ruler for drawing straight lines

#2 pencil and eraser

I like a pink eraser—the Paper Mate® Pink Pearl® eraser is my personal favorite.

Two fine point permanent markers

You need one black and one green or red or blue. The Sharpie® brand is my choice.

White Out

Correction fluid will "erase" any mismarks made with permanent markers.

Paper scissors

Clear plastic

You can use clear plastic to recreate a missing pattern piece or to redraw a shape. Cut open a sandwich-size or larger plastic bag. Place the plastic over the quilt top and trace the shape, copying any registration marks. Do not cut this plastic out; place it on a white surface, then place freezer paper over the plastic drawing. Tape it if necessary to keep it from slipping and copy the pattern shape onto the freezer paper. Cut the new freezer-paper pattern and iron it onto the right side of the fabric.

ScotchBlue™ Painter's Tape

Use this tape to hold your working drawing and fusible interfacing in place on your work surface while building your quilt. It will not leave a sticky residue.

Supplies for Constructing Your Quilt

Fusible interfacing

French Fuse, Fuzi-Knit, or other tricot, one-sided fusible interfacing used for knits are soft, drape well, and are more forgiving than other fusibles. They allow you to "edit" your work by gently pulling off an undesirable fabric choice and replacing it with a preferable selection. You need a piece 1"–2" larger than your paper design.

Fabrics

You can use fat quarters or smaller pieces. It's your choice as to how many different fabrics you want to use for your top. I like scrappy quilts, so if I run out of a certain fabric, I replace it with a different print of the same color and value.

Prewashing fabric

I use so many colors with light and dark values in the same quilt that it is necessary to prewash. I don't want the colors to bleed into each other. Mostly, I use printed fabrics. I love all the patterns and texture they give my quilts. Batiks are especially wonderful but they do need to be prewashed or at least soaked in the sink with hot water and rinsed until they run clear.

Usually, I go on shopping sprees and purchase a bunch of fabric at one time. I come home, separate the values, and wash the fabrics with a small amount of detergent and a dye catcher. I do not use fabric softener as it hinders sticking freezer-paper patterns to the fabric. I usually machine dry the fabric, but not completely! I take them out when still slightly damp and smooth by hand in a pile and allow them to finish drying flat. I do not iron the fabric until I am ready to press the freezer-paper patterns on that piece of fabric.

Don't stress about all your unwashed fabrics but start prewashing now as you purchase new fabrics.

In many class situations students come without prewashed fabrics. That's OK, but when they wash the finished project, I recommend using a dye catcher.

Storing fabric

I do try to sort my fabric by color family but I do not worry about going from light to dark. If all the greens (for example) are in the same general area, that's good enough for me. In fact, I think it helps to see a certain fabric if the colors aren't all mooched together. I purchase fabric with lots of pattern and contrasting color. Sometimes it's hard to determine where they should be stored. I just stuff them in with whatever seems to be the most dominant color.

When I purchase fabric I try to find some lights as well as the darks of a certain color. Whites that are not solid white are good to have on hand. Try to find some that have some soft blue, green, pink, or other colors in them. Even some old shirts might have a good value for your stash. What a novel idea from our pioneers in quiltmaking. Thank you very much!

Quilt backing

I recommend a muslin or solid color with a subtle print (no busy patterns) for backings. The design from the front of the top will emerge on the back as you machine quilt your creation.

28mm rotary cutter with Ann's Magic Button

Add ¼" seam allowance to all the pattern pieces as No Sewing Until You Quilt It is a turned-edge appliqué technique.

Ann's Magic Button adapts a 28mm rotary cutter to add an approximately ¼" seam allowance when you align the button on the cutter with the edge of the freezer paper as you cut out the pattern pieces.

I had the Pin Peddlers make my Magic Button with my logo (Fig. 1–1, page 11). It is available on my website www.AnnHolmesStudios.com, but you can make your own!

You need any ¾" plastic button with holes in it (not the shank type), a ⅜" square of double-stick foam tape, and a 28mm rotary cutter. **The 28mm cutter is used for all the projects in this book.** This is a great size cutter to use for rolling around all but the tiniest appliqué pieces (Fig. 1–2, page 11).

Trim the double-stick tape to fit the screw head on the blade side of the rotary cutter. Peel off the backing paper and press firmly to attach to the screw head only. This arrangement will not interfere with changing the blade.

Peel the transfer paper from the tape, center the button, and press firmly to attach it to the rotary cutter. This adaptation is important for rapidly adding seam allowances when using my No Sewing Until You Quilt It technique and is handy for other appliqué projects.

Fig. 1–1. Adding ¼" seam allowance with Ann's Magic Button

This button is not suitable when cutting pieces for precise, straight-line piecing. Stick to using your rulers.

Here is a photo of adapted cutters with both the 28 mm and a ¾" button and a 14mm rotary cutter with a ¼" button from my husband's shirt (Fig. 1–3). Use this smaller wheel for cutting the tiniest appliqué shapes.

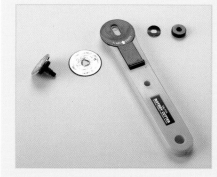

Fig. 1–2. 28mm cutter pieces

Sewer's stiletto

Clover makes both an awl and stiletto. I prefer the stiletto, which is longer and sharper. It has two useful functions: (1) to slide under the freezer-paper patterns to completely remove them; and (2), also very important, to lift the edges of a pattern piece without completely removing it. (You still need the pattern in place for lining up the next pieces but you don't want to have to pick paper out later that is stuck in the seam.) You can use bamboo-cooking skewers available at the grocery store, but these can break, so be careful with them.

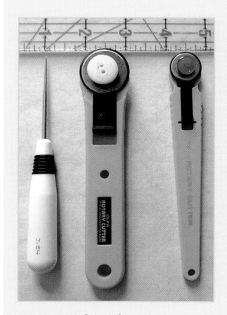

Fig. 1–3. Adapted cutters

Sharp-pointed small fabric scissors

An important tool— embroidery scissors are good.

Small paper scissors

Two glue sticks

Glue sticks must be fresh to easily glide onto fabric. Do not use tacky or sticky glue sticks. Use two glue sticks and alternate them to prevent them from drying out. I purchase the regular size clear Staples® brand for permanent mounting. It is acid free. Be sure to use *clear* glue sticks. You will need more than two for

Fig. 1–4. Sealing iron

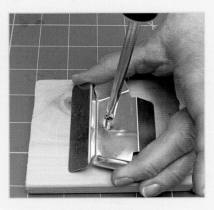

Fig. 1–5. Making the iron stand

larger projects. Apply glue with generous strokes, as this is what holds the seam allowances together until you stitch-and-quilt.

For detailed instructions for gluing your fabric pieces in place, see page 17.

Mr. Clean® Magic Eraser® Original

Glue will get on the bottom of your iron and turn brown. When your iron is cool, use this to remove the glue.

Standard iron and ironing board

Use these for pressing your fabrics and ironing freezer-paper patterns onto the fabrics.

Small sealing or appliqué iron

This iron is used as you "build" your quilt (Fig. 1–4). The 5" head of a sealing iron maintains its heat and provides more surface area to get the job done in a satisfying way with control. It can be purchased from www.towerhobbies.com or at your local hobby shop.

Iron stand

Sealing irons come with a small metal stand, but the metal gets hot and it's not very stable. Use a wood screw to attach the metal stand to a ¾" thick block of wood approximately 4" x 6"—an inexpensive and stable solution (Fig. 1–5).

Working surface

You need a flat surface for building your quilt top. It can be your dining room table or a folding table from a discount warehouse. These folding tables come in a variety of sizes and some have telescopic legs that will raise your table height to 36". You can always get bed lifters to raise your table to a comfortable height. A white surface is preferable.

Fear not about using an iron on a plastic table top as the working drawing, fusible, fabric, and freezer-paper patterns all come between the table and the heat of the iron. Do use a modified iron stand as explained above or use a hot pad under just the plain metal stand, as the metal alone can burn your fingers and or melt the plastic of the table.

Rotary cutting mat

Small gluing surface

You can use your tabletop to glue but I prefer to use a small (8" x 12") rotary cutting mat for gluing. It moves around with me as I work on a project and when it gets too sticky, I take it to the sink to wash off. **A small damp washcloth** is handy for sticky fingers.

Threads

Use invisible thread on the top and a light-weight bobbin thread. I like to use 60–wt. Superior® Bottom Line; 100–wt. silk; or 50–wt. DMC® thread in the bobbin to match the backing. I also like the more pronounced look of 40–wt. rayon embroidery thread in the bobbin, but the machine tension needs to be adjusted for this (see page 19).

Use clear invisible thread for light colors and smoke for dark colors. Invisible thread is both a blessing and a curse because it is invisible. I love it because stitching perfect stitches is not my strong suit. In addition, there is usually lots of pattern in my fabric choices and I do not need to add another design element by using thread with color. Do all of one color first, then do the second color all at once.

Beware! Invisible thread can wrap around the spindle and cause bobbin pops or perhaps break your needle. Stop and look at your spindle and machine. Is the thread wrapped around something that stops the flow? Be sure that the thread is coming off your spool in the correct direction. It never hurts to rethread your machine if you're having trouble.

There is a lot of invisible thread on a spool, but when it gets close to the end, I toss it out. Toward the end it seems more tightly wound and thus more curly and more apt to get wrapped around something to hinder my stitching.

Machine quilting gloves

Sewing machine and a free-motion foot

Machine needles

Use a new machine needle. My favorite is a Schmetz® #70/10 Metallic needle. I have used an 80/12 with great luck as it is a stronger needle but it leaves a bigger hole when stitching. After washing the quilt, however, holes made by the needle will close.

Cotton batting

I used Quilter's Dream 100 percent cotton batting for all the projects in this book.

Fabric spray adhesive

I use 505® Spray and Fix for basting the layers of the quilt sandwich because it has no unpleasant odor.

DVD

My (optional) instructional DVD, *No Sewing Until You Quilt It!,* is available at www.AnnHolmesStudios.com

General Guidelines: Dos and Don'ts

Use this section as a reference to review before each project.

Working drawing

The pattern printed from the CD is your working drawing and is left intact. It can be used many times. It's your road map for building your quilt top. Make a freezer-paper copy first, then lay the French Fuse over the working drawing and build your quilt top from there.

Each shape of the working drawing is numbered or lettered so that you know exactly where each piece belongs. Tape it to your work table with blue painter's tape.

Freezer-paper pattern

Cut freezer paper about an inch larger than your working drawing. Flatten the freezer paper by rolling it with shiny side out, then unroll and press on an ironing board with dry iron at a wool setting. It will easily peel off the ironing surface. Do NOT press it to the working drawing.

After it is flattened, lightly hold it in place over the working drawing with tape so it won't slip while you copy the pattern onto freezer paper.

Reproduce every line, number, and/or letter with a black marker. **Now add registration or tic marks** with a different color marker. These marks will help with correct placement of pattern pieces.

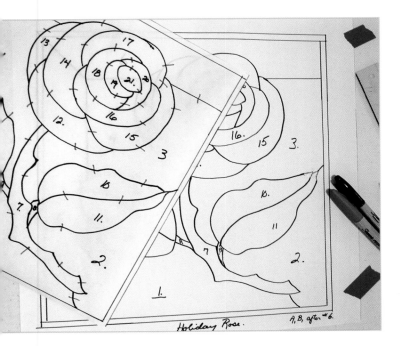

Note:

Please do not get "hung-up" on the numbering. The numbers must match between the working drawing and freezer-paper copy but that is not necessarily the order in which to build your project. There is usually more than one way to build, so relax! Soon, you will be deciding for yourself in what order you want to build. Note also that the numbers referred to in the how-to photos may not match the numbering on your printed pattern.

French Fuse

Cut one continuous piece of French Fuse about an inch or two wider and longer than the working drawing. Tape it over the drawing with the textured (adhesive) side up and the slick side down. The French Fuse should float over the drawing, taped only around the perimeter. Sometimes, my fingers are so rough from doing stained glass or gardening that it is hard to feel which side is which. But when you try to seal your first piece down and it doesn't stick, you'll know that you have to turn the tricot over! Not to worry—it will gently pull off the working drawing with no harm done.

Press patterns to fabric

Cut out freezer-paper pattern pieces on the lines with paper scissors. On small projects, I suggest cutting out all the pieces at once and placing them over the French Fuse in their proper places. This will aid you in selecting the right fabric for a particular piece. Simply pick up the pieces that will be all of the same fabric, make a stack, and place it off to the side to iron onto the fabric later. Continue selecting fabric and adding to the stack until you have all fabrics selected.

For larger projects, I prefer to cut pieces for one section at a time and attach them before going on to the next section. This helps keep track of pieces.

Use a dry iron to press the freezer-paper patterns to the RIGHT side of your fabrics. Usually a cotton or slightly lower temperature setting works best depending on your iron. A too-hot iron can melt the plastic coating and make it difficult to remove and reuse the patterns. It is just as important to have the iron hot enough to make the freezer-paper patterns adhere to the fabric. You can always iron the pieces down again if they come loose.

Position pattern pieces to be cut from the same fabric at least ½" apart. Cut out, adding ¼" seam allowance. See pages 10–11 for instructions on modifying your 28mm rotary cutter with Ann's Magic Button.

PART 1: Building Your Quilt Top— The Heart of the No Sewing Until You Quilt It Technique

All the pieces are positioned on the top before you stitch-and-quilt. Generally work from background to foreground, appliqué style.

Carefully place background pieces on the French Fuse, lifting the edges to see the lines on the drawing to ensure proper placement (Fig. 1–6, page 16). Fuse in place, leaving the paper pattern on the background fabric pieces. Seam allowances on many background pieces will NOT need to be turned under.

As you build (add pieces to your top), determine what edges need to be turned under. Hold the next piece that you want to place up to the French Fuse-covered drawing. Ask yourself, "Where will the edges touch?" Turn under only the edge(s) where the piece touches the previously placed piece(s). Seal down the new piece (Fig. 1–7, page 16). You will repeat this step with each piece that you add to your top, asking yourself again and again, "Which edges touch?"

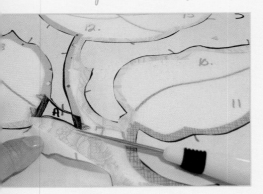

Fig. 1–6

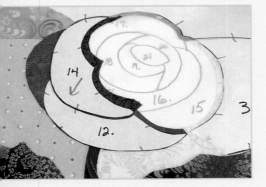

Fig. 1–7

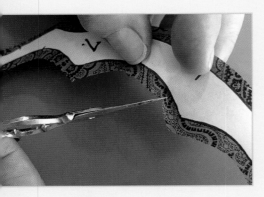

Fig. 1–8

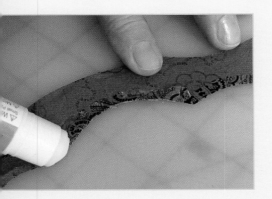

Fig. 1–9

Convex or outside curves will turn smoothly without clipping. Inside curves (concave) will require clipping to turn back smoothly. Carefully clip inside curves using small sharp embroidery scissors; clip to within a thread or two of the freezer-paper pattern, not into it, for a smooth edge (Fig. 1–8). Clip off any dog-ears that may stick out.

As you determine which edges of a pattern piece need to be finished edges, glue only one edge at a time so your fingers don't get sticky. Use glue stick only for the turned-under edges.

Apply the glue stick to the underside of the seam allowance and turn under. Finger press for a crisp edge.

Glue again, this time on the back of the turned-under seam allowance (Fig. 1–9). Both sides of the seam allowances are glued.

Position the piece over the extended seam allowance of the piece beneath, matching the registration marks and seal down.

Do not glue paper patterns together on the edges as you are building the top. You don't want to have to pick paper out of the seams. Lift pieces up with a sewer's stiletto. Apply glue liberally.

You'll notice how flat the quilt is as you are building. You won't have to worry about which way to press seam allowances as you would in traditional piecing. It is all built in with this method.

Continue building your quilt top using the registration marks for correct placement. Fuse as you go with the sealing iron.

Let the sealing iron do its work. Don't move it too quickly—you want to make sure that you are getting the fabric fused to the French Fuse foundation. Seal all seam allowances as well as the area under the freezer paper.

Remove the freezer paper only after surrounding pieces are placed. If you are not saving pattern pieces and you want to see the fabric, it is possible to tear the freezer paper leaving just the registration marks in place. Remove all paper after building the quilt top.

Gluing in 3 Easy Steps

HINT 1: Use fresh glue sticks.

HINT 2: Use a small cutting mat as a gluing surface that will move around with you and can be washed off in a sink. Keep a small damp washcloth handy for sticky fingers.

STEP ONE: Glue

Take your cut-out fabric piece with the freezer-paper pattern ironed onto its right side and place it freezer-paper side down on your gluing surface. Apply glue stick to the wrong side of the fabric on the seam allowance area only, gliding the glue stick in an outward motion toward the edge of the pattern shape. This direction of applying glue keeps the fabric from shifting and dislodging the freezer-paper pattern.

Pick up and hold the pattern piece with the freezer paper facing you. With your fingers in about the center of the edge that you are turning under, fold or roll back the seam allowance, pressing or pinching with your fingers and moving to the sides from the center in each direction. The freezer-paper pattern rules! The fabric must obey, or come close to obeying. You are gluing fabric to fabric, not fabric to paper.

Repeat this step on any other edges of the pattern piece to be turned under.

STEP TWO: Finger Press

Place the piece freezer-paper side up, and finger press the glued edges. This step ensures that the quilt will lie nice and flat.

STEP THREE: Glue

Now apply glue to the turned-under (the back of the) seam allowances. This edge is reinforced by the first gluing, so you can easily glide the glue along the edges of the seam allowance. Be generous with the glue; this holds the seam allowances until you are ready to stitch-and-quilt. Be sure to line up the registration marks and seal in place with the sealing iron.

As your quilt top grows you will have more space to use the flat of the iron to get a good seal to the French Fuse.

Edit your work when necessary. It is easy to replace a fabric choice if you are not happy with it. Gently pull off the offending piece by supporting the French Fuse with one hand as you lift off the piece with the other. You may have to pull back a few seam allowances to get it out. Cut a replacement piece, glue where necessary, and seal down.

Even after you have quilted the whole project it is still possible to patch-edit. This is possible because of my method of stitching around each shape—it will blend in.

Give the quilt top a final pressing with a regular size iron before making your quilt sandwich. Pressing is done with up and down movements, not moving the iron sideways, which might lift pieces.

Remember to unplug your irons when you are finished working.

Remove the top from the working drawing (Fig. 1–10).

Fig. 1–10

PART 2: Stitch-and-Quilt

So many people who finish a traditionally made quilt top wonder, "How am I going to quilt this?" With my technique, you will know exactly how to proceed.

How much quilting is necessary? Quilting on Quilter's Dream Cotton, which I recommend, can be as much as 8" apart. Do as much or as little as you feel comfortable doing.

First prepare your quilt sandwich. Cut backing fabric and batting about 2"–4" inches wider and longer than the finished project. Tape the backing to a table so that it won't shift.

I recommend 505 Spray Baste. Spray the backing. Place your batting on top. Spray the batting and position your quilt top. It is helpful to fold the batting and/or top in half, or in quarters on larger quilts. Then unfold to lie flat, being careful not to stretch the batting layer. Don't square up yet, but do trim the extra batting and backing. You don't want sticky residue on your sewing machine. No pins are necessary to hold the quilt sandwich together.

Plan your work and hand movement. Decide which direction to stitch first. The free-motion foot lets you travel in any direction. You can put the needle down and turn your work when necessary to "go at it" in a better direction.

Now you are ready to stitch-and-quilt. Because there is no sewing in it at all, the first thing to do is to secure all the pieces by stitching through all the layers with a straight or zigzag stitch. If you do straight stitching, stitch very close to the edge. I like to use a small zigzag stitch (1.5 or 1.6). After the quilt is washed, the stitches sink into the batting, and the quilt looks more like a pieced quilt.

Stitch-and-quilt with the free-motion foot or darning foot. Drop your feed dogs for added ability to move in any direction. It is not necessary to stitch around every single piece because pieces underneath will be held down by the pieces on top.

Complete your outline and echo quilting in one section before moving the quilt to another area, especially if it is a large project.

If you decide to quilt with the zigzag stitch, and you want your stitches to go in another direction from the one your machine stitches, set your machine to straight stitch and move the quilt top with slight hand movements to create your own free-motion zigzag stitching. Stitch in the ditch or between the pieces to travel to next section. The more you stitch around a piece, the more it pops out.

Keep a sewer's stiletto handy to hold down design edges that might lift as you are stitching. The stiletto can also be used to push under a seam allowance that might have sneaked out.

Threads and tension

Keep a practice quilt sandwich by your machine to test what the stitching looks like before you begin on your masterpiece. Make it with the same fabrics and batting as your project.

Tension adjustments are sometimes necessary when using invisible thread to get an even stitch. You can tighten the bobbin tension on machines with an eye on the bobbin case by threading the bobbin thread through the eye or simply lower the upper tension if the bobbin thread comes to the top of your quilt. A lower setting

number usually indicates lower tension. Check your machine's manual.

Once you figure out the right combination of thread and needle, be sure to keep the thread flowing freely. (See page 13 for specific recommendations on threads and needles.)

Starting and stopping

To start quilting correctly, bring the bobbin thread to the top of your quilt. This keeps the back looking neat and prevents dragging unclipped threads into the stitching. Hold onto the top (invisible) thread and take one stitch with the presser foot down. Now, lift the presser foot and tug on the top thread and a loop of bobbin thread will come to the top. Pull it all the way through to the top, then hold it with the top thread while you take a few small stitches to lock them in. Clip both threads, leaving a neat beginning.

Ending takes a bit more practice, but is well worth it, as it will keep your work very neat on the back of the quilt. First take a few small stitches and raise the needle to its highest position. Lift the presser foot and pull the quilt about 6" toward you. Holding the top thread, slide the quilt back under the needle. Lower the foot and, while keeping hold of the top thread, take one down and up stitch close to the last stitch taken. Raise the foot again and tug on the top thread to pull the bobbin thread up to the top of the quilt. Cut both threads close to the quilt top. Curved-tip scissors cut surface threads nicely, without as much risk of cutting the quilt top.

Thanks to Linda Fiedler for teaching this technique in one of the first machine quilting classes that I took.

Projects

TULIP WITH HEART, 16" x 16", made by the author with assistance from Julie Bagamary, Marie Marcella, and Helen McCarthy, all from the Asheville, North Carolina, area

TULIP WITH HEART:
Learn How, Step by Step

This simple little project will walk you through the process that is used in all the projects in the book. Several samples were made of this block. Stitch-and-Quilt is Ann's preferred method to finish her quilts but Marie hand appliquéd a block after it was glued and sealed before making the quilt sandwich. She slip-stitched around individual pieces and the needle slipped through quite easily. However, for hand applique you must hand stitch around the outside edges first, working your way in so that the block is not disturbed by being bunched up in your hands. If some pieces lift off, just glue and press them down with an iron.

General Supplies

Freezer paper
Ruler
#2 pencil and eraser
Two different color fine point permanent
    markers
White out
Small paper scissors
Painter's tape
Sewer's stiletto
Sharp-pointed small fabric scissors
Small paper scissors
2 glue sticks
28mm rotary cutter with Ann's Magic Button
Sealing iron (best) or small appliqué iron

For a detailed description of these supplies, see pages 8–13.

Yardage

10 fat quarters
    You can use fewer if you decide to
    repeat a fabric.
French Fuse – 17" square
Backing – fat quarter
Batting – 18" x 18"
Binding – ⅛ yard

Get Ready

Prepare Your Design

Print the pattern from the CD. This will be your working drawing. You will build your quilt on top of this. Do not cut it up. It remains whole and you can use it again and again.

Notice that there is a narrow edge around the perimeter of the design. This marks the outside edge and allows a little extra room for squaring the quilt after you stitch-and-quilt. Notice also that each piece of the design has a number.

Prepare the Freezer Paper

Tear off about an 18" length from the roll of 18" wide freezer paper. To remove the curl from the freezer paper, re-roll it in the opposite direction (shiny side out). Then heat your regular iron to the silk/wool setting and press waxy-side down on your ironing board. Do not iron freezer paper to the working drawing.

Make the Freezer-Paper Patterns

a. Lay your working drawing on a table and use blue painter's tape to secure it. It will stay in place until your top is completed.

b. Position the freezer paper on top of the working drawing with a few more pieces of blue tape to hold it in place (Fig. 2–1). You should be able to see through the freezer paper to the design below. You could tape it to a window during daylight hours or use a light box if you have trouble seeing the pattern clearly.

c. With a black permanent marker carefully trace the design onto the freezer paper. Be sure to copy the numbers and all borders.

d. Make registration marks WITH A DIFFERENT COLOR MARKER. (If you use the same color as the pattern shapes, you may get confused as to what the shape is, especially on patterns with many small pieces.) These little tic marks will help you position the pattern pieces as you build the quilt top.

e. Remove the freezer-paper copy.

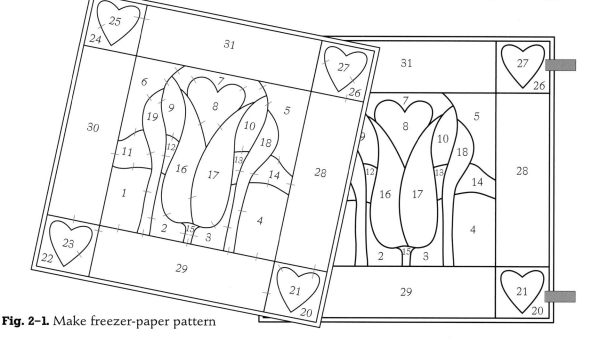

Fig. 2–1. Make freezer-paper pattern

Get Set

French Fuse

Cut a piece of French Fuse about an inch or two larger than the pattern on all sides. Tape it over the working drawing with the fusible side up (texture side up, slick side down).

Cut out the freezer-paper patterns. Note that the corner blocks have floating hearts in the center (no line connects the heart to the edge of the square). To make cutting easier, cut through from the bottom edge of the heart shape but leave the square intact with the slit.

With paper scissors, trim the outside perimeter of the quilt pattern and discard the edges of freezer paper. Extend the pattern lines into the margin, since the margin is not a separate piece, but an extension of the edge pieces. The inside line is the finished edge of the quilt. The outside line is added to allow some room for squaring your project AFTER you stitch-and-quilt.

Cut out all the individual shapes and lay them on top of the French Fuse in the corresponding position on the design.

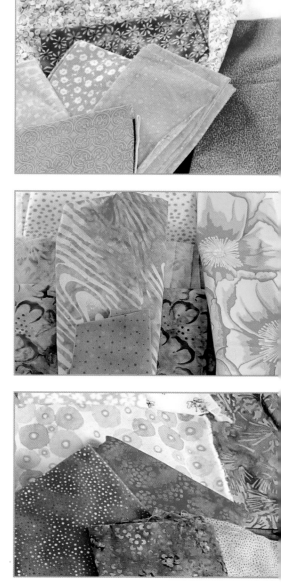

Go

Now lay your fabrics close to your working drawing and decide what color goes where (Fig. 2–2). Pick up the pattern shape that goes with a certain fabric and just lay it on top of the fabric choice for now. Once you have a stack of fabrics and pattern pieces, take them to your ironing board.

Press the fabric and iron the freezer-paper patterns to the RIGHT side of the fabrics. Leave about ½" of space between pieces on the same piece of fabric (Fig. 2–3).

Cut off a hunk or section of fabric so you're not working with an unwieldy large piece. With a cutting mat under your work, rotary cut each piece by rolling the magic button along the edge of the freezer-paper pattern. It will give you approximately a ¼" seam allowance.

Fig. 2–2

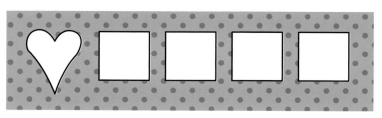

Fig. 2–3

Fig. 2–4

Fig. 2–5

I am right handed so my rotary cutter is in my right hand. With my left hand I can help move the fabric into my cutter when going around curves (Fig. 2–4). With a little practice you will soon find out how quickly you can cut out all your pieces.

When all your pieces are cut out you are ready to start building your quilt. *Leave all the freezer paper on the cut out shapes; that is your guide for building* (Fig. 2–5).

Background

Take all the background pieces (#1–#7 and #9–#14) and place them nearby.

Turn on your sealing iron to one setting below the high mark and place on a stand.

Position piece #1 on the fusible, matching its position to the drawing. Carefully lift the seam allowances to see if you have positioned the pattern correctly within the lines of the drawing beneath the French Fuse.

When you are happy with its position, use the sealing iron to fuse in place, using the point of the iron to go around all seam allowances and inside the shape. French Fuse is more forgiving than other fusibles but try not to get your iron on the naked fusing material. Don't worry that it doesn't seem to be doing much. Just touch the freezer-paper pattern to see if it feels warm. The quilt top is "floating" over the drawing and if the iron is hot enough, it's working! *Leave all the freezer-paper patterns attached to the fabric until instructed to remove them.*

Continue to position and seal down all the freestanding background pieces (#2, #3, #4, #5, and #6) with their seam allowances extending into the next pattern area (Fig. 2–6).

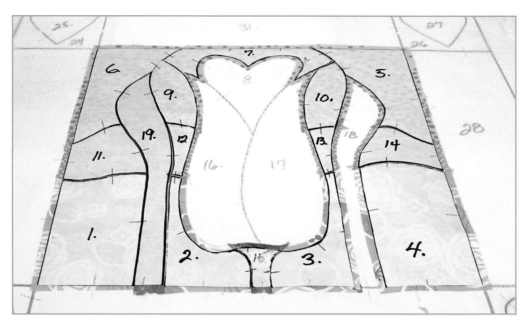

Fig. 2–6. Background pieces with seam allowances extending into next pattern areas

Turned-under Edges

Now we will need to start turning under the edges that touch as we continue to build.

On curved pieces, clip ONLY the inside curves; clip even if it is only a slight inside curve. Clip into the seam allowance ONLY to the edge of the freezer paper (leave a thread or two of space) not beyond, or you will have a choppy looking curve. We aim for nice smooth edges.

Take piece #11, hold it up to its position, and ask yourself which edges need to be finished. That's right—you need to turn under only the top and bottom of #11, as those should be finished edges. The sides to the right and left of #11 will have other pieces on top. You should clip any inside curves.

See page 17 for detailed instructions on the 3 steps for gluing the seam allowances.

Glue the top and bottom edges of #14 and fuse in place.

Next do #7. Hold it up to the drawing and see what needs to be turned under—just the edges that would touch #5 and #6.

Next come #9 and #10. Now it's time for an extra step. When you hold up #9 you can see that only a small section at the tip of the shape needs to be turned under. Hold up #9 to #6 and #7, and see where they touch. Make a clip or notch, and turn under from the point to the clip or notch. Turn one edge at a time. Fold the second side back and clip off dog-ears after both sides are turned under.

Follow the 3 steps of gluing for the edges of #9 and #10 only where they touch #6, #7, and #5. Fuse in place. Then glue only the top and bottom edges of #12 and #13. That's all of the background. Fuse in place.

The Tulip

Now look at the leaf (#19). Hold it up and see that all of the edges except the bottom of the leaf should be turned under. Glue and finger press one edge at a time and clip off any dog ears that stick out. Keep it flat.

Please, never bunch extra fabric under. Fold it smoothly to the pattern shape and if it sticks out, just cut it off. Remember to do the second gluing (the undersides of all seam allowances). Then seal down to the French Fuse.

Place the next leaf (#18) like you placed #19, then do the stem #15 turning under only the sides.

Next comes #8, the heart shape. Hold it up to quilt top and see what needs to be turned under. You can see that only the top half of the heart shape needs to be a finished edge. The bottom half will have #16 and #17 on top. Use your scissors to clip in the seam allowance at the location where it changes from being a turned edge, leaving the seam allowance exposed. Clip just to the freezer-paper edge.

When you clip, never clip into the paper or the edge will appear choppy.

Now clip into the dip in the heart only to the paper edge, so that you can turn back the edges smoothly. Remember to turn under from the center outward.

Next is #16. Turn under the edge only along the left side where it touches #9, #12, and #2. Once you have turned the left side, hold the piece up to the quilt and note where it touches #7 and #8. Turn and glue that edge. The remainder of #16 will remain unturned, since it will be covered by #17. Glue and seal into position (Fig. 2–7).

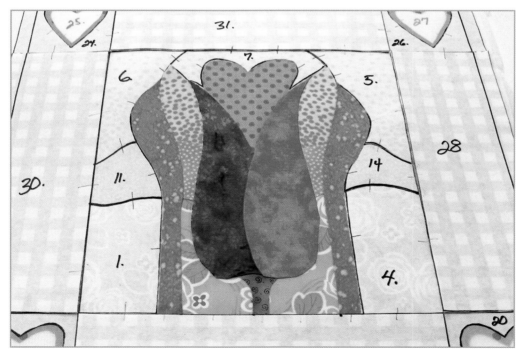

Fig. 2–7

Turn under all the edges of #17 and seal down. Remember that you seal each piece to the French Fuse as you add a piece to your quilt top.

Add your first border piece #29 by turning under only the top edge. Fold to the edge of the paper so that you form a straight line!

After you add borders #30, #31, and #28, turning only the long edges that surround the center part of the design, you can remove pattern pieces #1, #11, #6, #7, #5, #14, and #4. Now it's time to add the corner blocks by turning under the 2 inside edges of each block that touch the rest of the quilt.

Quilters like to see their fabric; so at this point you can slide your sewer's stiletto under the freezer-paper patterns to uncover all of the inside sections only (pieces #2, #15, #3, #13, #10, #9, #12 and #19).

Finish the corners by placing the hearts. Only one clip into the center dip of the heart is necessary. Turn back the edges and secure with a glue stick on the back of the seam allowances.

Remove all freezer paper. Your quilt top is ready to be sandwiched with batting and a backing (Fig. 2–8).

See the Stitch-and-Quilt instructions, pages 18–19.

Fig. 2–8

HOLIDAY ROSE, 15" x 15", made by the author with assistance from Julie Bagamary and Helen McCarthy

HOLIDAY ROSE

I took a simple rose and adapted it for the No Sewing Until You Quilt It technique by adding two borders and connecting the lines with the edges, creating individual shapes for the background.

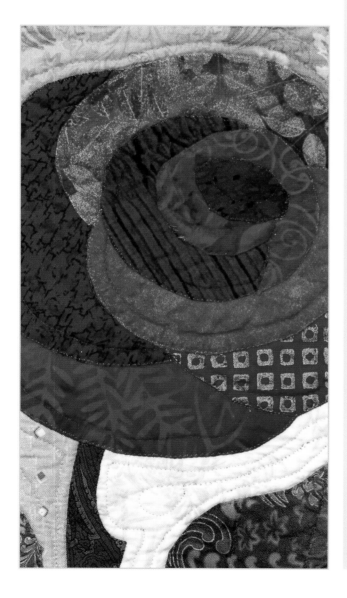

General Supplies

Freezer paper
Ruler
#2 pencil and eraser
Two fine-point permanent markers
White out
Small paper scissors
Painter's tape
Sewer's stiletto
Sharp-pointed small fabric scissors
Small paper scissors
2 glue sticks
28mm rotary cutter with Ann's Magic Button
Sealing iron (best) or small applique iron

For a detailed description of these supplies, see pages 8–13.

Yardage Requirements

Flower—red scraps
Leaves—green scraps
Stem—brown scraps
Background—2 fat quarters neutral
Backing—1 fat quarter
Batting—18" x 18"
Binding—⅛ yard
French Fuse—17" square

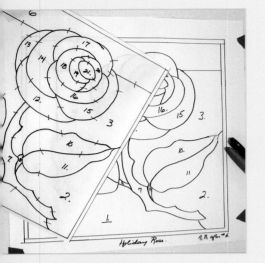

Fig. 3–1

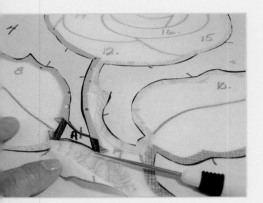

Fig. 3–2

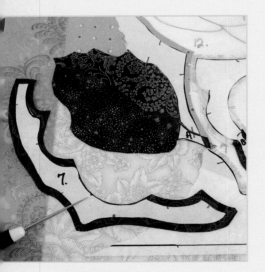

Fig. 3–3

Print the pattern from the CD. Cut an 18" x 18" piece of freezer paper and copy the working drawing onto it. Include numbers, the tiny letters A & B, and the outside perimeter lines. Add registration (or tic) marks and extend the pattern lines into the perimeter. Tape the pattern (your working drawing) to the table (Fig. 3–1).

Cut out the freezer-paper pattern shapes with paper scissors. Press the patterns onto the right side of the fabrics, spacing them at least ½" apart. Cut out with scissors adding ¼" seam allowance or rotary cut using the Magic Button.

Place French Fuse over the drawing, textured (adhesive)-side up.

The numbers on this pattern indicate the sequence for fusing the pieces in place.

Position #1, carefully lifting the seam allowances to check for correct placement (Fig. 3–2).

Find where #2 touches #1 and turn only that edge under using the 3-step gluing method (page 17).

Where #3 touches #2, turn the edge.

There are turned edges on #4. Fuse it into position.

The border is considered part of the background so position #5, turning the edges that touch #1 and #4 only, and seal down. Turn #6 where it touches #3, #4, and #5 to finish the background.

For the center stem, start in the middle area and clip inside curves to the freezer paper. Glue only one little section of the inside curve at a time and turn back. Then, do the opposite side and the bottom of the stem. Clip off any dog ears that stick out. All edges should be turned except the top of the stem where it tucks under a rose petal (Fig. 3–3).

Next, do the larger pieces of the leaf #8 and #9.

The 2 tiny stem pieces lettered A and B are slight inside curves. Clip them to the edge of the freezer paper so they will turn under smoothly. **Do not clip into the freezer paper as that leaves a jagged look to the finished piece.**

When doing these small pieces, the working drawing all but disappears under the seam allowances of the neighboring pieces. Fear not. This is where the little tic marks come in handy and just the glue will hold the pieces in place.

Do the tops of both leaves, #8 and #10. Turn only the top edges that touch background. A vertical clip may be necessary to prevent exposing an unfinished edge. Turn under all the edges of the bottom halves of the leaves, #9 and #11.

Now you are ready to build the rose from the outside petals in, #12–#21. Work from back to front. Place #13 first, then #12, #14, and #15. Alternate the shades in the petals to give the rose definition. Clip the corners of the petals as you go where necessary to keep them from peeking out (Figs. 3–4, 5, and 6).

One little tail was sticking out but it was easy to pull up the adjacent petals and readjust their positions to cover them (Fig. 3–7).

Eureka—it is not often that I finish a piece that I am completely satisfied with.

I am happy with the assortment of colors. Remember to alternate the shades in the petals to give it definition.

Make your quilt sandwich to stitch-and-quilt.

See the Stitch-and-Quilt instructions, pages 18–19.

I will now wax philosophical. We are so hard on ourselves. I am often my own worst critic. Perfection is a hard and not very happy road to travel. Relax—with No Sewing Until You Quilt It, you have the opportunity to make adjustments and then move on. Take what you have learned to the next project. Happy Quilting!

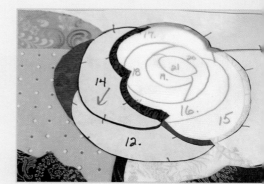

Fig. 3–4

Fig. 3–5

Fig. 3–6

Fig. 3–7

LET PEACE BE OUR COMPASS, 24" x 24", made by the author

LET PEACE BE OUR COMPASS

I made this in Egypt on my daughter's dining room table, starting one week after Mubarak was ousted. The stitch-and-quilt was completed in Arlington, Virginia.

General Supplies

Freezer paper
Ruler
#2 pencil and eraser
Two fine-point permanent markers
White out
Large paper scissors
Painter's tape
Sewer's stiletto
Sharp-pointed small fabric scissors
Small paper scissors
2 glue sticks
28mm rotary cutter with Ann's Magic Button
Sealing iron

For a detailed description of these supplies, see pages 8–13.

Yardage

Fat quarter EACH of light, medium, and
   dark blues
Fat quarter EACH of light and dark gold
Scraps of red and purple
Fat quarter of white and scraps of 2 other
   off-whites
Fusible interfacing—26" x 26"
Backing—⅞ yard
Batting—28" x 28"
Binding—¼ yard
French Fuse—27" square

Building the Background

Print the pattern from the CD. Study the line drawing. Generally we begin with the background but by saving the larger pieces of the inside of the sun and the blue outside corners for later, it will give a smoother curve than if we had lots of little pieces for those edges. So, begin by placing the triangle pieces inside the radiant ring.

In building this project do not follow the numbers. The numbers are only for identification and placement. When you copy this design onto the freezer paper to make your pattern pieces, be careful to copy the numbers in the same orientation! The little triangular shapes are easy to turn a wrong way. Notice that just the tips of some of the triangles need to be glued and turned back so that no raw edges are exposed (Fig. 4–1).

Lift seam allowances to see the line on the drawing for careful placement. Clip off any fabric (for example, on #89 and #90 at the top of the circle) that might overlap.

Seal the blue and purple triangles as you place them around the radiant ring. The inner radiant ring is completed first. Place every other triangle, then continue building. You can start almost anywhere on the circle of triangles. I chose to start with #47 and work up and around the circle.

#60 and #61 form one triangle at a tail feather so turn one of the edges where they are joined (Fig. 4–2).

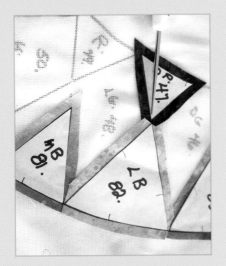

Fig. 4–1

Fig. 4–2

Hold #45 up to #84 and you will see that you need to turn under the long edge of #45 where the two pieces touch (Fig. 4–3).

Next, place #44. Turn under the long edge that touches #45, and just the tip that touches #43.

Now, place #40 by just turning back the opposite tips where they touch #43 and #38.

Place #37, turning back the edges where it touches only #38 and #89.

Skip #41, #32 ,#59, and #50 until later. They will be easier to do after placing the corner rays, and will finish the inside edges of #30, #31, #28, and #29.

Continue around, asking yourself what touches, and turn under the appropriate edges or tips of pieces (Fig. 4–4).

Relax and follow the directions. We are skipping around, but there is a method to this madness; all will be revealed!

As you can see in figure 4–4, we placed #91 and #70, leaving # 34, #32, and #67 until later. Next it is fun to place #8. You can see how it covers seam allowances and smooths out the curve.

In figure 4–5 we have positioned a large corner piece #99 first. It is turned under only on the inside curve, creating a nice smooth line. Hold up #98 and you will see that it needs a bit of clipping and turning only in the pointy end so that no raw edges will show. Notice that we leave #28 open until later. Keep building around the outside of the circle, leaving open the yellow corner rays. Now, you can prepare the corner rays by gluing and turning under only one edge at a time; remember the paper pattern rules. By gluing only one edge at a time and letting it "set" while preparing the other pieces, it will firm it up a bit and have a crisper turned point. (Too much glue at one time will make the point slip out of shape.)

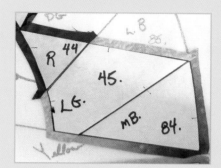

Fig. 4–3

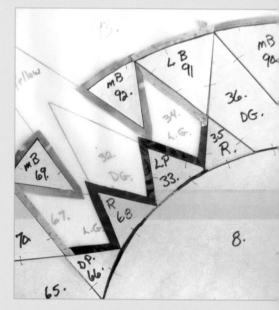

Fig. 4–4

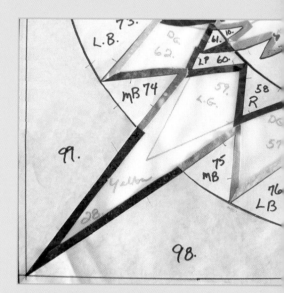

Fig. 4–5

Carefully, just slightly roll back the last edge of the tip that you turned, and use very sharp embroidery scissors to clip off the dog-ear that sticks out beyond the tip. Sometimes it helps to let the glue dry a bit before clipping. Go ahead and prepare all those spiky pieces (#24– #31) in this same manner. (Notice that on #24 there is a slight indentation for one of the olive leaves; just fold fabric straight across the dip.) Then do all the clipping of the sharp points at the same time; that will give the glue a moment to dry before clipping.

Finish placing the background pieces that make up the sun. Place #4. It requires no turned edges; just seal it down. Do #5; you only need to turn the curved edge. Proceed by holding the next pieces up to the adjoining piece to determine if there will be a finished edge. If it touches somewhere, a clip is needed to ease in turning back that section of the piece. Go ahead and do the olive leaves, turning edges around all sides. After the top is completed, sat-in stitch with colored thread to provide the stem of the branch.

OK, back to the opposite end of those corner spiky pieces (#28–#31). This is easier than it looks. Before applying any glue, hold the piece in its position and look and see that only the top flat tips of the end need to be folded back (photo area 6, top right corner). You can see in photo area 7 that you can remove freezer-paper patterns when they are no longer needed to define the placement of the adjoining piece. All the background is in place (Fig. 4–6).

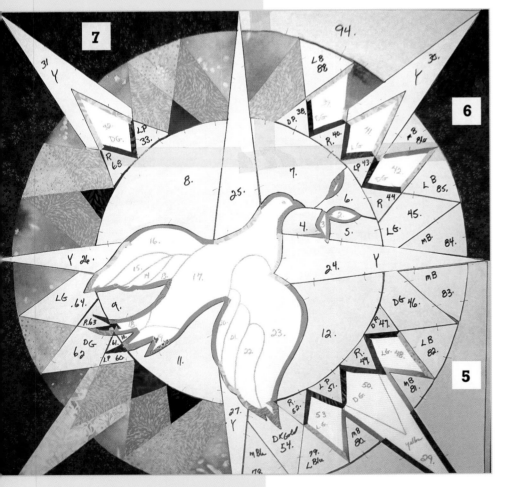

Fig. 4–6

Building the Dove

The back wing #16 is where to start building the dove (Fig. 4–7). Clip inside curves only in the slight dip on the top part of the wing. Turn under the top of the wing and also a small section on the tip of the wing, where it touches #9 and #64, and put it in place. Give the same treatment one piece at a time with #15, #14, then #13.

Next, work on the main body of the dove. Hold up #17 to the design and determine where it has to be turned under, including the part that touches background piece #11. Be sure to give a clip to the top of the beak; it will define its shape.

Fig. 4–7

Wing #23 in the foreground should be prepared next and sealed down. Then follow with the other wing segments #20, #21, and #22. Work by turning under the back edges and coming forward, turning under all around #22.

Cut into the deep V of the tail feathers and turn under. Do #18 first, then #19.

See the Stitch-and-Quilt instructions, pages 18–19.

And you're done! Spread your wings.

Study your future designs and decide the best approach for building. Because there is no sewing it gives you the freedom to adjust your design. My motto is, "Go ahead and give it a try!"

SPRING LANDSCAPE

SPRING LANDSCAPE, 14" x 27", made by the author with assistance
from Marie Marcella and Helen McCarthy

SPRING LANDSCAPE appears to be very simple yet it has some fun challenges. You will gain confidence and skill as you complete it.

For shading of the white dogwood flowers and water, use both the front and back of your chosen fabrics.

The pattern from the CD can be enlarged, making some of the tiny pieces easier to work with. Note that lots of registration marks were added. It makes it easier to build with everything in the correct location.

General Supplies

Freezer paper
Ruler
#2 pencil and eraser.
Two different color fine-point permanent
    markers
White out
Large and small paper scissors
Painter's tape
Sewer's stiletto
Sharp-pointed small fabric scissors
Small paper scissors
2 glue sticks
28mm rotary cutter with Ann's Magic But-
    ton
Sealing iron (best) or appliqué iron

For a detailed description of these supplies, see pages 8–13.

Yardage

Hills, mountains, and foliage—½ yard TOTAL a variety of greens and blues (The largest pieces can be cut from fat eighths.)

Water—¼ yard TOTAL a variety of blues (You'll need a long quarter for the longest piece. The other pieces can be cut from fat eighths or scraps.)

Tree—⅛ yard TOTAL a variety of browns

Dogwood blossoms—scraps of light print fabric

Border—⅛ yard light green

Border squares and binding—¼ yard dark green

Backing—½ yard

Batting—18" x 31"

French Fuse—16" x 29"

If your fabric choices have direction, as in the sky and water and the tree fabric, it's wise to put an arrow with a third color marker (so you don't confuse all the lines) on the corresponding freezer-paper pattern pieces, indicating the direction that you want to use.

Building Sequence

Print the pattern from the CD for your working drawing. Trace onto freezer paper, add registration marks, and cut out the pattern pieces.

Press the pattern pieces to the RIGHT side of your selected fabrics and cut out, adding ¼" seam allowance.

Helpful Hint:

When rotary cutting out the fabric for the small petals, make the seam allowance just a bit smaller than ¼" by moving the edge of the magic button to just inside the edge of the freezer-paper pattern. There will be less bulk to turn under.

Build the sky down to the water's edge and the water up to the land. Next, place the border pieces, as the tree and flowers come out over the border. Be on the lookout for the tiny border piece labeled A. It is hidden down between a piece of grass and the tree trunk.

This part goes very fast and you can't wait to place the next pieces. It will slow down as we build the tree and then the flowers; so you might want to take a break (Fig. 5–1).

Build the tree from the ground up. Place the branch in the back, come forward with the other branches, then place the tree trunk. Do the dogwood flowers next, working around the centers. Here you can pull off the freezer-paper patterns you no longer need as placement guides (Fig. 5–2).

The flower petals are pretty small at the size I made this design, so make sure that the patterns are attached to the fabric. If the pattern is loose it is frustrating to glue properly with the fabric shifting around. Just re-press the pattern to the fabric.

I thought that I had lost one of my petals and was prepared to remake the missing piece when I decided to check the fabric that I used. Sure enough, there was the missing piece still attached to my fabric. I just forgot to cut it out!

Give a final pressing and make your quilt sandwich to stitch-and-quilt. I did minimal quilting on this project—mostly just outline stitching because of its small size.

See the Stitch-and-Quilt instructions, pages 18–19.

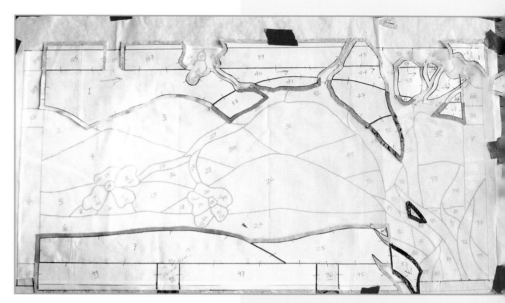

Fig. 5–1

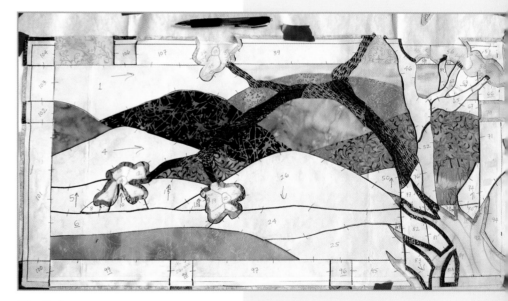

Fig. 5–2

ORIENTAL IRIS TRIPTYCH

ORIENTAL IRIS TRIPTYCH, 34½" x 47½", made by the author
with assistance from Julie Bagamary, Helen McCarthy, and Diana Ramsay

Three 15½" x 34½" panels are joined to make a wallhanging or wall screen.

I admire Oriental art and I enjoyed using my stash of Oriental fabrics for this project. It is pretty wild but I had fun with it. This triptych was designed as a landscape; you could select fabrics that would more realistically depict sky, distant mountains, water, ground, and rocks.

General Supplies

Freezer paper
Ruler
#2 pencil and eraser
Four different color fine-point permanent
    markers
White out
Small paper scissors
Clear plastic
Painter's tape
Sewer's stiletto
Sharp-pointed small fabric scissors
Small paper scissors
Several glue sticks
28mm rotary cutter with Ann's Magic Button
Sealing iron (a must on larger projects!)
24" square rotary ruler or carpenter's square

For a detailed description of these supplies, see pages 8–13.

Yardage Requirements

Lantern—fat quarter red

Purple iris—2–4 fat eighths purples (Use the back of some of the fabrics for shading the petals.)

White iris—scraps of light-colored fabric

Stamens—fat eighth gold lamé

Foliage—½ yard TOTAL a variety of greens

Background—¾ yard TOTAL EACH light, medium, and dark prints

Backing—1½ yards (2¼ yards if it is a directional fabric)

Binding—½ yard

French Fuse—3 pieces 16" x 35" EACH

Batting—3 pieces 18" x 38" each (cut from a twin batt)

Building Sequence

Print the pattern from the CD for your working drawing. Trace onto freezer paper. To help with organization of which pieces go where, use a different color marker for the registration marks on each of the three panels (for example, orange on the left panel, blue on the center panel, and green on the right panel).

Fig. 6–1

Cut out the pattern pieces.

If you have tabletop space, it's great to be able to work on the background for all three panels at the same time (Fig. 6–1). Otherwise, I suggest you work on the center panel first because you can test the colors in the flower without cutting out too much fabric.

Build the background from top to bottom. Next build rocks under the lantern from the bottom to the top.

Continue building up for the lantern. That was fun. Now the iris get to be more complicated, but you can do it.

Some shapes have deep cuts into the pattern pieces (as on #210 and #233) but since you don't have seams to sew, they're easy to do. It is very easy to do these shapes, as you don't have to worry about sewing seams (Fig. 6–2).

Place your pattern pieces close to where you will be using them. This saves from having to hunt them down one at a time. Note that the leaves are built from the top down, because they are in back and we build to the front.

Fig. 6–2

Helpful Hint:

Cotton fabrics usually turn under beautifully with no fuss, but I used some cotton lamés for some of the iris leaves and a satin polyester ribbon for the iris beards; these are very springy fabrics.

To make it easier to turn under those specialty fabrics, add another step to your gluing process.

First, as always, clip any necessary inside curves to within a thread or two of the freezer paper. Spread the glue on the seam allowances that need to be turned under and then set the piece aside without attempting to turn the edge. Let the glue dry for a few minutes while you work on placing another piece or two.

Come back to the springy fabric piece and glue the same edges again, then turn them under. The dried glue will have stiffened the fabric a bit to allow it to lie down nicely.

Give a final pressing to each of the panels and make your quilt sandwiches to stitch-and-quilt (Fig. 6–3, page 47). See the Stitch-and-Quilt instructions, pages 18–19.

Joining the Panels

Please read all the way through before trimming the edges of your panels. Make sure that you have completed the stitch-and-quilt before trimming the panels.

Use your working drawing to determine the correct finished edges of the quilt. First, cut the panel pattern along the inside drawn line, removing the added perimeter to establish the FINISHED edge of the panel.

Lay the pattern for the first panel directly on top of the matching stitched-and-quilted panel. Line up some of the design lines in the quilt with short straight pins pushed through the paper. With a blue water erasable marker, make dash marks along the LONG SIDES ONLY of the paper onto the quilt panel underneath. Remove the pins and paper. Position a long straight ruler ¼" beyond the blue line and trim with a rotary cutter.

Repeat down the SIDES ONLY on the remaining two panels.

Position the quilted panels side by side on a flat surface, overlapping the added ¼" seam allowances. Use blue painter's tape to line up the design. Notice how the lantern does not appear to line up. Most of that difference is sewn into the binding and will disappear.

This is where you can shift the panels up or down if needed. That is why the tops were not

Fig. 6–3

Note:

If you use binding strips wider than 2", you will have to make the connecting pieces a bit wider than the 1½" called for.

trimmed yet. With the panels lined up as you like, take a 24" square, position along a straight side, and with your water-soluble marker, mark the top and bottom edges of your quilt and trim. On the top and bottom, just try to get the panels square. It is not necessary to add extra seam allowance.

Cut 9 – 2" wide strips for the binding. Join with 45-degree seams. Press the seams open. Fold the strip in half lengthwise, wrong sides together, and press.

Attach the binding to all 4 sides of the 3 separate panels but do NOT turn and finish.

To make the connecting pieces, cut 4 binding strips on the straight of grain 1½" wide and the length of the panel sides minus ½". Place two strips right sides together and sew a ¼" seam across both short ends. Turn wrong sides together and press, forming a connecting piece of two thicknesses. Pin down the center of the strips to hold them together. Repeat with the other 2 strips (Fig. 6–4).

Fig. 6–4. The front of the panel shows the narrow binding attached, while on the back of the panel you can see the wider connecting strip attached.

Determine the correct sides of the panels to be joined. Stitch a double strip to the back of the right edge of the first panel following the same stitching line that you used for attaching the binding to the front. Stitch the same connecting piece to the back of the left edge of the next panel. Be careful to fold the top corner of binding out of the way so that it doesn't get caught in the stitching.

In the same way, joint the third panel.

Hand or machine finish the binding, folding the panels back out of the way for stitching.

BLOOM WHERE YOU ARE PLANTED, 90" x 90", made by the author with assistance from Julie Bagamary, Helen McCarthy, and Rachael Smith

BLOOM WHERE YOU ARE PLANTED

I made this quilt for my world-traveling daughter, Amy, with more than a little help from my friends. Julie was new to building a quilt top without sewing but she is an accomplished machine quilter. Rachel had never done any machine quilting until she worked on this quilt. It is a great project to work on as a group.

There are seven large blocks, so seven different people could each stitch-and-quilt a block. The side blocks (30" x 30") and rectangular sections (45" x 30") along the top and bottom are each made twice, so working in teams of two on those repeated sections is another option.

You can both cut out the freezer-paper patterns, then take turns ironing the freezer-paper patterns onto the fabric selections and rotary cutting with the Magic Button. The vine border is not as difficult as it might appear. Building with a friend, it will go pretty quickly. Organization is key to working efficiently.

Save the freezer-paper patterns as you remove them so you can use them again on the repeated sections (Fig. 7–1). Separate the vine from the background pieces.

The units are joined after they have been quilted.

General Supplies

Freezer paper
Ruler
#2 pencil and eraser
Two different color fine-point permanent
    markers
White out
Large paper scissors
Clear plastic
Painter's tape
Sewer's stiletto
Sharp-pointed small fabric scissors
Small paper scissors
A box of glue sticks
28mm rotary cutter with Ann's Magic Button
Sealing iron
3 – 8½" x 11" full sheet labels

For a detailed description of these supplies, see pages 8–13.

RIGHT **Fig. 7–1.** Removed freezer-paper patterns

Yardage

Fabrics

1 yard EACH 3 different hot pinks (3 yards total)

½ yard EACH 6 lighter pinks, medium to pales and white with pink (3 yards total)

6 fat quarters greens (for leaves)

1 yard green (for the narrow borders)

9 yards total for the background of creams and off-whites, and white-on-white patterns

8½ yards backing cut as follows:

3 pieces 34" x 34"

4 pieces 34" x 48"

98" x 98" batting to be cut to fit each section

¾ yard binding

French Fuse:

3 pieces 32" x 32"

4 pieces 32" x 46"

Preparing the Pattern

Print the pattern from the CD for your working drawing. Draw an additional perimeter line on the drawing ¼" beyond the finished pattern edge on all sides of each pattern section. Copy both of the perimeter lines onto the freezer paper when you're making the pattern. When you rotary cut with the Magic Button you will also be adding another ¼". This will give approximately ½" extra all around the design for squaring up the block sections after quilting. You will use the center panel pattern once and use each of the other patterns twice.

You will notice in (Fig. 7–2) that I forgot to put in my registration marks on this section. I got ahead of myself. When you get excited about a new project it is easy to just forge ahead. I was

Fig. 7–2

still able to build my top but it would have been easier to have the registration marks.

Building Sequence

30" Side Blocks

Begin by building the two 30" side blocks. This will warm you up for the 30" x 45" blocks.

Position and seal down every other square block (the dark ones) in the border; it is not necessary to turn any edges. Then place the light-colored blocks, turning under just the sides that touch the dark squares. At the corners you will have to make small clips and turn back a small area where the light and dark squares touch.

Build the background portion next. The pieces are large and it will go quickly. It will go faster still if you build from the outside vine border toward the center of the quilt. That way there is no clipping involved, as all the edges that need to be turned are outside curves! Continue building along the diagonal. After the large center background pieces are in place, build the big Rose of Sharon flowers.

Start with the green leaves that touch the flower. Turn the 2 edges of the leaf that are touching the background (Fig. 7–3). After placing those leaves, turn under the two long edges of the stem that goes to the bud. Place the rosy part of the bud, then place the short petal, then the longer petal to finish the bud.

Build the flowers from the outside in, as we did with the HOLIDAY ROSE design. It goes very quickly with no clipping, as you are only turning the outside curves. Place every other piece first (Fig. 7–4).

On the next tier, place every other piece first. The petals in between will be turned on the two side edges (Fig. 7–5).

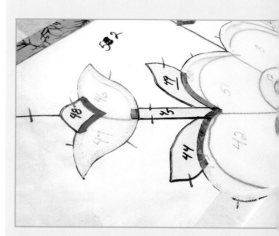

Fig. 7–3

Fig. 7–4

Fig. 7–5

Fig. 7–6

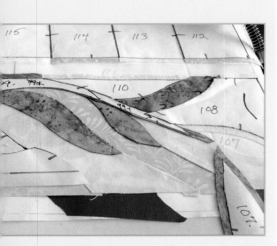

Fig. 7–7

To make nice round circles for the center of the flowers, I traced around different sizes of thread spools. Draw these circles on printable full-page labels for the computer because they have a sticky back and are a bit firmer than regular paper. Stick the label to the back of your fabric; it will stay inside the quilt. Use a glue stick to turn back the edges around the shape; it will be easier to make a nice round shape with the paper inside. After gluing the right side of the label, use your stiletto to spread or even out the gathers when the glue is still moist. Don't worry—it washes just fine (Fig. 7–6).

Helpful Hint:

As you complete a section and remove the pattern pieces, save them to use again on the duplicate sections. Do NOT mix all the quilt pattern pieces together or you'll make yourself crazy! Keep the pattern pieces from each unit together until you're ready to do the second sections. Sort them in shallow boxes and try to separate them by the parts in the section.

Vine Border

To build the vine border, start with the background pieces, then the leaves (except the end leaf that covers the stem). Two clips at the top of stems (like #99) will allow green 1" border pieces to pass over without the interfacing showing through (Fig. 7–7).

Most of #99 is turned under, except for a small section that touches the green border. Two clips into the seam allowance at the top of #99 (where part of the pattern arches up to the green border) will allow a flap of seam allowance to be exposed. This will be covered by the green border that frames the vine border without any of the French Fuse peeking through.

When placing the heart, start by clipping into the dip and turning back the top edge. Wait to place rest of the heart until the green border piece is down. The next piece of the heart will give a nice curved finish.

30" Center Block

Place the background pieces first, building from the outside edges toward the center. Next seal down the very center of the large flower. Now turn under the side edges of the green direction points and start to build the flower from the outside in toward the center (Fig. 7–8).

The spirals are fun and fast to do. I started with letter R and built one after the other around the circle, turning under the curve There is no clipping when working in this direction (Fig. 7–9).

Be sure to have enough color contrast in your fabrics to make all this work pop. I replaced a lighter pink for this dotted fabric because after stepping back and looking, the design of it almost disappeared (Fig. 7–10).

Stitch-and-Quilt

Make a quilt sandwich as you finish each block.

IMPORTANT: Note on the diagram that where two sections are to be joined, 2" of space must NOT be quilted along one of the edges to enable joining the sections later. This preserves 2" of space for turning the edge and joining later. **Use a walking foot to sew a basting stitch through all the layers of the quilt sandwich about 2" from the edges** as indicated in the quilting plan (Fig. 7–11, page 54).

Stitch-and-quilt, starting and stopping without crossing the basting lines. Do not travel along the basting lines. The quilting stitches will be continued after the units are joined and the basting stitches are removed.

Fig. 7–8

Fig. 7–9

Fig. 7–10

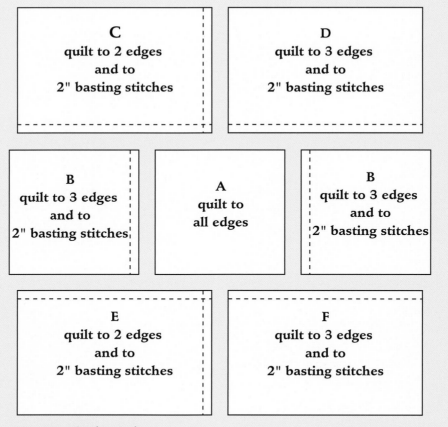

Fig. 7–11. Quilting plan

Helpful Hint:

Quilting three sides of the 2½"
squares up to the corners, then traveling
back from the corners along the bottom
of the row of squares makes for a neater
appearance and saves quilting time (Fig.
7–12).

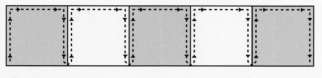

Fig. 7–12

Joining Side Blocks to the Center Block

Square up the center block (Unit A) using the 2½" squares as a reference point. **The
other blocks will be squared AFTER they
are joined, not before.** Using a long ruler,
measure ½" from the outside edges of the
blocks. (That ½" includes a ¼" seam allowance and a ¼" clearance between the block
and the seam that joins the blocks.)

Depending on how much shrinkage that
you have from machine quilting, the block
should square up at approximately 30½" x
30½" inches.

Joining the Units

Determine the finished edge of the quilt units by checking your working drawing. Keep it handy to refer to for the actual size of the finished units—the inside perimeter of the pattern.

Helpful Hint:

The small 2½" squares are key to finding the edge of your quilt. Use a 3" x 5" or 4" x 6" note card and draw a line 2½" from a long edge. Take this to your sewing machine with the quilt section and place the card on your quilt at the left-hand edge of the row of blocks and baste along the right edge of the card. This marks the finished edge of your quilt.

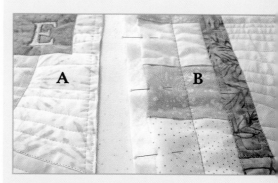

Fig. 7–13

On the center Unit A that was quilted all the way to the edges, baste through all layers ¼" from the edge of the quilt with matching thread. This provides a joining line (Fig. 7–13).

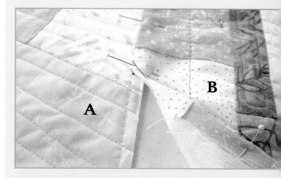

Fig. 7–14

On the edge of Unit B with the basting line that preserved 2" of clearance, gently pull the top of the quilt away from the batting and fold the backing and batting out of the way. Secure with safety pins.

Use a glue stick and turn under the quilt top seam allowance on Unit B along the edge to be joined to Unit A (Fig. 7–14).

Position Unit B along the finished edge of Unit A. Use straight pins to hold it in place. With a walking foot, invisible thread, and a narrow zigzag or straight stitch, sew the top layer of Unit B through all layers of Unit A (Fig. 7–15).

Fig. 7–15

You can see by this photo of the back of the quilt how the batting was held out of the way while stitching the top of the second unit to the whole sandwich of the fully quilted, center unit (Fig. 7–16).

Remove the pins and gently separate the backing from the batting. Lay Units A & B on a flat surface with the top face down. Flatten out by pressing with your hands. Keep the quilt backing folded

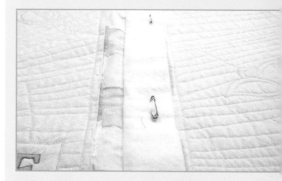

Fig. 7–16

Fig. 7–17

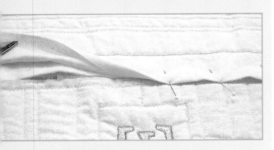

Fig. 7–18

Fig. 7–19

Fig. 7–20

Fig. 7–21

back out of the way. Trim the batting of Unit B to be flush with Unit A (Fig. 7–17).

Fold under the backing of the quilt along the stitching line, without glue this time, as you will have to adjust it as you move along the length of the unit. Pin in place, just covering the stitching line (Fig. 7–18).

If you're not using invisible thread, be sure your top thread matches the back and the bobbin thread matches the front of your quilt. Zigzag stitch through all layers. Remove the basting stitches that preserved your margin of clearance, and finish stitching and quilting through all the layers with a free-motion foot. Repeat with the second B unit.

After you join the A and B units, it is time to square and trim off any excess (Fig. 7–19). Measuring out from the 2½" inch blocks plus ¼" for a seam allowance will give you the correct line (Fig. 7–20).

Join Units C & D along the center seam, again leaving a 2" margin free on one of the edges. (See the quilting plan, page 54). The bottom edge of BOTH units needs to have the 2" unquilted area for joining to the A & B units.

Similarly, join Units E & F, then add to the A & B units to complete the quilt top.

When I joined the two large bottom units, there was a part of the center flower that was uneven, so I made a patch for it. I simply turned under a new piece with the glue stick, pinned it in place, then zigzagged with invisible thread on top around the shape. Then I turned the quilt over and this time had invisible thread in the bobbin and pink on top and followed the echo line that was done originally. This is called patch-editing (Fig. 7–21).

Bind the quilt, then wash to remove the glue.

To dry, spread it out on a large table or the floor with a large sheet of plastic underneath. Use a 15" square ruler to make sure the center block is square.

SUMMER'S END, 90" x 90", made by the author with assistance from Rachel Smith, Helen McCarthy, and Julie Bagamary. Longarm machine quilted by Brian Fackler.

SUMMER'S END

Hummingbirds filling up for their long migration before the end of summer and rich fall colors beginning to appear were the inspiration for this quilt. It was made in five sections and longarm machine quilted.

The 44" x 44" center medallion could be a stand-alone project. Satin stitch done in colored thread was used to make the beaks and vines before the unit was sandwiched. Inspiration for the curly border design came from a stair railing in the Natural History Museum in Washington, D.C.

When people see my quilts, I am often asked, "How long does it take?" Rachael, my college-aged assistant on this project, timed us. It took 38 hours for the two of us working together, from cutting out the paper pattern to the finished center medallion. Later we spent some time editing the pieces that we wanted to change.

After I established my fabric choices, three of the big border units were built on dining room tables in Kansas and Missouri during a long visit with relatives. When the table was needed for dining, a plastic tablecloth was put over the top of the quilt! The quilt top returned to North Carolina to be longarm machine quilted by Brian Fackler at ThreadPlay.com. He can stitch right on the edges of each individual piece as his hand control is on the hopping foot of his machine, not by handlebars up in the air (see photo, page 59).

General Supplies

Freezer paper
Ruler
#2 pencil and eraser
Two fine-point permanent markers
White out
Large and small paper scissors
Clear plastic
Painter's tape
Sewer's stiletto
Sharp-pointed small fabric scissors
Glue sticks (You'll need many for this large project; they come 18 in a box.)
28mm rotary cutter with Ann's Magic Button
Sealing iron
Package of 1" round white mailing seals or price stickers

For a detailed description of these supplies, see pages 8–13.

Yardage

½ yard EACH of 14 different autumn colors for the brick-like outside border and around the center medallion (7 yards total)

¾ yard EACH 6 yellows – light to deep golden for around the border and center medallion (4½ yards total)

½ yard purple for inner borders

3 – 4 fat quarters of greens to blue-greens for hummingbirds

½ yard EACH of 5 different greens light to dark for curly Qs and vine leaves (2½ yards total)

5 fat quarters in shades of orange for the trumpet flowers (1¼ yards total)

Scraps of ruby red for hummingbird throats and flower centers

French Fuse:
    1 piece 46" x 46"
    2 pieces 24" x 46"
    2 pieces 24" x 92"

8¼ yards backing
98" x 98" batting
¾ yard binding

Brian Fackler at ThreadPlay.com

Building Sequence

Let's begin by building the background in the center medallion (Fig. 8–1). You should be very comfortable with the building technique by now. Finish with the small inner border and then the larger ring (Fig. 8–2). Go for it and enjoy!

By building every other ray toward the center, you will not need to turn any edges on the outer pieces, and you only need to turn under one overlapping edge of every inner pattern piece that you add. Then fill in with the alternate rays, turning two edges on the outer pieces and three edges on the inner ones. The big circle ring will finish it nicely.

Fig. 8–1

Fig. 8–2

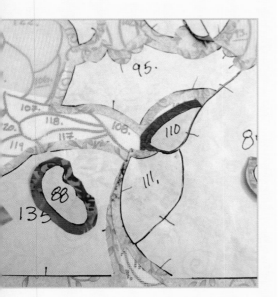

Fig. 8–3

Hummingbird Building Sequence

Place belly first, then the throat and head. Build the tail feathers from the longest to the smallest. Then do the tiny piece under the wing span and build up, finishing with the larger uplifted part of the wing (Fig. 8–3).

Satin stitch the beaks and vine details.

Helpful Hint:

Take close-up photos of the intricate areas of the design—because as you build the quilt the seam allowances will cover up many of the numbers and the photo will serve as a helpful guide.

Curly Q Building Sequence

Place the background pieces first in whatever portion of the drawing will fit on your work surface (Fig. 8–4). Reposition the drawing and quilt top as needed.

To build the curly lines, begin at any one point and move along in an order that makes sense to you. Then do the flowers, finishing with either the cap piece on the trumpet flower or the round center.

I used 1" round white price stickers purchased from an office supply store to make nice round circles. These stickers will stay inside the circles. Position the sticker on the wrong side of the fabric and use a glue stick to turn back the seam allowances. Use lots of glue to attach the circles to the quilt.

Fig. 8–4

As you complete a section and remove the pattern pieces, save them to use again on the duplicate sections. You might want to save the center design pieces to use again for a 44" square wallhanging.

The second time around will go much faster just by looking at the fabric choices you have already made and checking the numbers on your drawing. Just pick up the curled pattern and place it on top of the fabric. After you've made your stacks of fabrics and pattern pieces, iron the pieces onto the selected fabrics. They will flatten out and you are ready to use your Magic Button again.

By working this way, it will give your quilt a kind of symmetry, as the second long side will be turned to the opposite side of the quilt (Fig. 8–5). If one or two of the curled-up pattern pieces goes missing—no worries! Just make a new pattern piece using a clear plastic sandwich bag (see page 9 for details).

Satin stitch the hummingbird beaks and the vines as before.

Joining the Units

Because this project was longarm machine stitched-and-quilted, the whole quilt was joined into one large unit. From your working drawing determine the finished edges of the units to be joined. Add ¼" beyond for the seam allowance. Sew the 2 short borders to the top and bottom of the center medallion square. Press the seam allowances open. Before joining the long side borders, pull back the green Curly Q vines about an

inch or two and pin them back out of the way. Stitch the long seams and press the seam allowances open.

After sewing the seam, make a bridge over the seam with the existing vine or an added vine for a smooth join.

If you decide to quilt this on your home sewing machine, stitch-and-quilt it in the five separate units, then follow the instructions in BLOOM WHERE YOU ARE PLANTED for joining the quilted sections (pages 51–56).

See the Stitch-and-Quilt instructions, pages 18–19.

Fig. 8–5. Shows editing detail: Pieces were gently pulled from the French Fuse. A new piece was inserted and glued where necessary and then sealed down.

Finishing Your Quilt

Square Your Quilt

For a large quilt I often place a large cutting mat on top of the quilt as a big square with another mat underneath. Use a marking pen to mark your edge, then cut along the line with a straight ruler and rotary cutter.

Bind Your Quilt

Yardage given for binding assumes straight-of-grain strips 2¼" wide, joined with 45-degree angle seams. You will need more yardage for bias-cut binding. Use your favorite method to apply the binding.

Sewing down the binding by hand is a joy for me. It is like a reward to have gotten to this point and I can cuddle with my quilt while relaxing, usually watching a movie. Remember to stretch your arms and hands once and awhile, as repetitive motion is not good for us. Take breaks.

Wash Your Quilt

Washing will remove glue, shrink up all the stitching holes, add texture, and soften the quilt.

I use a washing machine, cool water, and a dye catcher). Presoak for about 10 minutes to soften the glue. Follow the manufacturer's instructions for the batting that you used. For example, the Quilter's Dream Cotton Request that I used in these projects can be gently machine washed in cool water and dried on the lowest heat setting using a static control dryer sheet.

While the quilt is still wet I will usually remove it from the dryer and lay it flat to dry. I put a large plastic sheet on the floor and pat it out with my hands to manipulate it into a square.

Label Your Quilt

Minimum information on a quilt label should include your name, where you live, and the date. Any other information would be helpful for future historians: for instance, the techniques you used and the type of batting.

Meet Ann Holmes

Ann Holmes, stained glass artist and quilter, has been producing site-specific stained glass since 1976. Public glass commissions include several churches and the 8½' skylight in the Lyon business building in Batesville, Arkansas. In Asheville, North Carolina, she designed and built windows for the Asheville Area Arts Council and the Grove Park Inn. In 1999, Ann became involved with the Asheville Quilt Guild and had a desire to recreate some of her original glass designs into fabric without the lead line look of stained glass quilts.

As a stained glass artist Ann was accustomed to building her windows on top of a drawing. Ann approached her quiltmaking in the same way, building her quilt tops on a fusible tricot interfacing as a foundation placed directly over her drawing.

Ann prefers the look of a turned edge, so she applied what she learned from hand appliqué to include the background where every patch or piece in her designs is built using a glue stick to turn the edges instead of using needle and thread.

In the early stages of developing her technique, she would build a small section of the top, then take it to the sewing machine to stitch. In 2005, foot surgery forced her to think of a new method to finish her project to meet the deadline for the Asheville Quilt Show. She asked herself,

"Why am I sewing this twice, once for stitching the top and a second time for quilting?" No Sewing Until You Quilt It, my turned under appliqué technique, was the result.

Ann was invited to give her first demo of her technique to her Asheville quilt guild in February of 2006, and she has been teaching her method ever since. AQS published her Daylily pattern in the November 2008 issue of *American Quilter* magazine.

Ann is a past school board member for the Stained Glass Association of America. You can see her website at AnnHolmesStudios.com and order her DVD and Magic Button to adapt your rotary cutter to easily cut appliqué pieces with a ¼" seam allowance.

Her RAINBOW FALLS stained glass piece was the first design she made with her new technique. (See the CD for both the stained glass piece and the quilt it inspired.)

More AQS Books

This is only a small selection of the books available from the American Quilter's Society. AQS books are known worldwide for timely topics, clear writing, beautiful color photos, and accurate illustrations and patterns. The following books are available from your local bookseller, quilt shop, or public library.

#8663

#8670

#8665

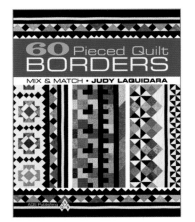

#8662

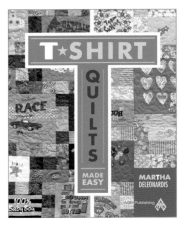

#8664

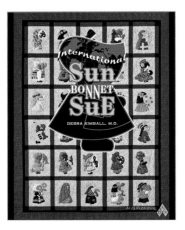

#8347

#8529

#8523

#8532